My Fair Lady

ALAN JAY LERNER

Level 3

Retold by Derek Strange
Series Editors: Andy Hopkins and Jocelyn Potter

T0345849

Pearson Education Limited
Edinburgh Gate, Harlow,
Essex CM20 2JE, England
and Associated Companies throughout the world.

ISBN: 978-1-4058-8195-1

Published in Great Britain by Max Reinhardt and Constable 1958
Published by Penguin Books Ltd 1959
This adaptation first published by Penguin Books Ltd 1997
Published by Addison Wesley Longman Ltd and Penguin Books Ltd 1998
New edition first published 1999
This edition first published 2008

9 10

Text copyright © Derek Strange 1997
All rights reserved

My Fair Lady is based on *Pygmalion* by George Bernard Shaw.
Used by permission of the Public Trustee and the Society of Authors.

The moral right of the adapter has been asserted

Typeset by Graphicraft Ltd, Hong Kong
Set in 11/14pt Bembo
Printed in China
SWTC/09

Acknowledgements
The publisher would like to thank the following for
their kind permission to reproduce their photographs:
Rex Shutterstock: Warner Bros 3, 5, 8, 18, 20, 22, 24, 27, 29, 31, 33, 36, 37
Cover images: *Front and back:* **Shutterstock.com:** Masson; **CD Cover:** *Onbody:*
Shutterstock.com: Masson

Published by Pearson Education Ltd

*Every effort has been made to trace the copyright holders and we apologise in advance for any unintentional omissions.
We would be pleased to insert the appropriate acknowledgement in any subsequent edition of this publication.*

For a complete list of the titles available in the Pearson English Readers series, visit
www.pearsonenglishreaders.com.
Alternatively, write to your local Pearson Education office or to Pearson English Readers
Marketing Department, Pearson Education, Edinburgh Gate, Harlow, Essex CM20 2JE, England.

Contents

Introduction

'After just six months with me,' said Professor Higgins, 'you'll be able to go to dances with the richest people in London – and they'll never guess where you're from!'

Professor Higgins is interested in language and accents. When he meets Eliza Doolittle in a London street, he doesn't just see a poor young flower-seller; he hears an interesting London accent.

In those days – the first half of the 1900s – accents were more important than they are today. Poor people with strong local accents never mixed with rich people with 'good' accents. So Eliza could only ever work in the street because of her accent.

The professor asks himself: can he teach a girl like this to speak differently? Can he teach her to be a lady? The professor's friend Colonel Pickering thinks it is impossible. He is so sure that he makes Higgins an offer: if Higgins can change Eliza into a lady, Pickering will pay for all her lessons.

The musical *My Fair Lady* was first seen in 1958 in London, and the film was made in 1964. Eliza Doolittle was played in the film by Hollywood star Audrey Hepburn, with Rex Harrison as Professor Higgins.

The story of *My Fair Lady* is really older than this. Alan Jay Lerner took the story from the play *Pygmalion* (1912) by the Irish writer George Bernard Shaw and added songs to it.

Alan Jay Lerner wrote the words for the songs in *My Fair Lady*, and Frederick Loewe wrote the music. Their songs are still loved around the world. You can read the story and the songs in this book, or just the story. The songs have some difficult language in them. If you want to understand them better, there are special notes at the back to help you.

Chapter 1   A Terrible Accent

It was a cold March night in the centre of London. It was raining heavily. Eleven o'clock: the theatres were just ending and crowds of theatre-goers in their fine evening clothes were coming out on to the wet streets. In Covent Garden,★ rich Londoners were leaving the Royal Opera House★ and walking across Covent Garden square, looking for taxis. Some of them stopped and stood talking together for a few minutes in front of St Paul's Church,★ on one side of the square. Near the church a group of fruit- and vegetable-sellers were warming themselves round a small fire before they started their night's work at Covent Garden market. Three street musicians were singing and dancing; some of the crowd stopped to watch them. Shouts of 'Taxi! Taxi!' cut through the noise of the crowd and the icy night.

Freddy Eynsford-Hill, a rich-looking young man of about 20 years old, pushed his way through the crowd round the dancers; his mother was just behind him. They were looking for a taxi, too. Suddenly, one of the dancers knocked into Freddy and he jumped back, but by mistake he knocked over a young woman, a flower-seller at the market, and she dropped some of her flowers on the ground. That was how Freddy first met Eliza Doolittle.

Eliza was then about 18 or 20 years old, and she was not a very good-looking young woman. She was wearing a dirty little black hat, a not-very-clean white blouse, an old skirt and old shoes; she had not washed her hair for several days and she clearly needed to visit a dentist.

Eliza stood up quickly and looked angrily at Freddy, then at her flowers, lying on the ground.

★ Covent Garden, The Royal Opera House and St Paul's Church are all real places in central London.

1

'Aaaooowww, you . . . !' she shouted at him. The crowd turned to watch and listen.

'I'm so sorry,' Freddy said, going red in the face, and he tried to pick up some of the flowers.

But Eliza went on rudely, 'That's two bunches of my flowers all dirty now. A lot of money, that is. Why don't you look where you're going?' She had a very strong London accent.

But Freddy's mother had no time for this young flower-seller's problems or her London accent – she just wanted to get home. 'Go and find us a taxi, Freddy,' she ordered him.

'Sorry, Mother. I'm going now,' and he turned and disappeared into the crowd, with another quick 'Sorry' to Eliza before he went.

Eliza turned to the older woman. 'So he's your son, is he? Well, he's knocked my flowers all over the ground and now he's run away without paying.'

Freddy's mother gave Eliza an unpleasant look, turned away and followed her son through the crowd with her nose in the air.

Talking unhappily and not very quietly to herself, Eliza got down on her knees and started to pick up the flowers. One of the fruit-sellers got down next to her and said quietly, 'Be careful. There's a man over there who's writing down every word you're saying. Maybe he's a detective . . .'

Some of the people near them heard this and turned to look at the man, standing on the outside of the crowd. He was busy writing in a small book and he did not look up. Eliza was frightened. 'Hey! I haven't done anything wrong, speaking to the gentleman about my flowers, have I? I'm a nice girl. I only wanted him to pay for my flowers.' And she started to cry.

Some of the people in the crowd, immediately on Eliza's side, told her not to worry, to stop crying. The man with the little book stopped writing and came over to her.

'It's all right, it's all right,' he said. 'Nobody's hurting you, stupid girl! Who do you think I am?'

Talking unhappily and not very quietly to herself, Eliza got down on her knees and started to pick up the flowers.

'I promise . . . I never said a word . . .' Eliza cried.

'Oh. Stop it! Stop it now! Do I look like a policeman?' the man asked, in quite a friendly way.

'Then why are you writing down all my words?' Eliza asked. 'How do I know what you wrote about me? You just show me what you wrote.'

The man opened his little book and held it under her nose.

'What's this? That isn't real writing. I can't read that,' Eliza said.

'But *I* can,' the man answered, and he started to read from his book, pronouncing the words in the same way that Eliza pronounced them with her strong London accent. ' "Well, he's knocked all my flowers over and now he's run away without paying." See? But why are you in this part of London – you come from west London, don't you?'

Eliza was frightened again. How could this gentleman know

3

where she came from? She started to get angry again. 'Why can't I leave the west? Why can't I come to work here, eh? I'm a good, hard-working girl, I am. And you're no gentleman, trying to make trouble for a poor girl like me.'

But the people in the crowd were interested in the man now, and another gentleman asked him how he could know where Eliza came from.

The man with the little book turned to him. 'I study phonetics – the different accents of English and other languages. That's my job. I can easily hear if people come from Ireland or Yorkshire,★ and I can hear which part of London people come from, too. I can often tell you which street they're from.'

Eliza cut in. 'Well, you look after your business and leave me to look after mine, then . . .'

Now the gentleman started to get angry. 'Woman! Stop being so rude to me, or go and find another church to stand in front of. Your English accent is absolutely *terrible* – it hurts my ears to hear it. God has given you our wonderful language, and you use it like an animal!'

Eliza did not know what to say, so she just said, 'Aooooow!'

'Aooooow?' the man repeated. 'What kind of word is that? Oh,' he went on unhappily, 'why can't the English teach their children how to speak? People in every other country teach *their* children to speak their languages well, so why can't the English do the same?' He looked carefully at Eliza for a minute, then turned and spoke to the other gentleman in the crowd. 'You see this person with her street accent, her street English that will always keep her in the street? Why can't she work in some rich person's house or in a good shop? Why can't she go to fine parties and dances? I'll tell you why: because of her accent! All she needs is six months' study with me and . . .'

★ Yorkshire: part of the north of England where people speak English with a local accent.

4

'Aooooow?' the man repeated. 'What kind of word is that? Oh,' he went on unhappily, 'why can't the English teach their children how to speak?'

Eliza was interested. 'Here, what's that you're saying?'

'Yes, you,' the man turned to her. 'After just six months' study of our language with me and you'll be able to go to dances with the richest people in London – and they'll never guess where you're from!'

Eliza liked this idea. She turned to the other gentleman. 'Aoow! *You* don't believe that, do you?'

'Well, it *is* possible,' the man answered. 'I study the languages of India, so I know a little about it, too.'

The man with the little book was immediately interested. 'Do you, sir? Do you know Colonel Pickering, the writer of those books on Indian languages?'

The gentleman smiled. 'I *am* Colonel Pickering,' he answered. 'And who are you, sir?'

'I am Professor Henry Higgins, the writer of *Higgins' Universal Alphabet*.'

Colonel Pickering was very pleased. 'Professor Higgins! I came from India specially to meet you!'

'And I was planning to go to India to meet you!' Higgins answered. The two men shook hands warmly.

'You must come and stay with me, Colonel Pickering. I live at 27a Wimpole Street. Come along with me now and we can talk over some supper.' The two men started to walk away, but then Higgins remembered Eliza and threw some money to her.

She picked up some of the money. 'Aaaah-ow-ooh!' she said and quickly picked up the rest of it, getting more and more excited. Then she ran over to the people near the fire to show them the money. They laughed with her for a minute or two about all her money at last turning her into a real lady, then she moved into the shadows near the church and started singing to herself. One by one the others turned and listened to her singing.

> *All I want is a room somewhere,*
> *Far away from the cold night air;*
> *With one enormous chair . . .*
> *Oh, wouldn't it be loverly?*
>
> *Lots of choc'late for me to eat;*
> *Lots of coal makin' lots of heat;*
> *Warm face, warm hands, warm feet . . .!*
> *Oh, wouldn't it be loverly?*
>
> *Oh, so loverly sittin' absobloominlutely still*
> *I would never budge till spring*
> *Crept over me winder sill.*

Someone's head restin' on my knee,
Warm and tender as he can be,
Who takes good care of me . . .
Oh, wouldn't it be loverly?
Loverly! Loverly!
Loverly! Loverly!

Suddenly a cold wind blew across the market square and they all remembered where they were, who they were, and that it was nearly time to start their night's work – they moved back to the fire and warmed their hands.

Chapter 2   A Little Bit of Luck

Later that evening, at a pub not far from Covent Garden, Eliza's father was in a bit of trouble, too. The barman was throwing him and two of his friends out of the pub – they didn't have enough money to pay for their drinks.

'Come on, Doolittle. If you can't pay for it, you can't drink it. I don't give it away, you know. Out you go now.'

Alfred Doolittle, still wearing his dirty old work clothes, came out into the street, looking quite unhappy.

'Well, thanks for being so kind, George,' he shouted back at the barman. 'Send the bill to Buckingham Palace!'*

Just then Eliza came round the corner. Her father's face broke into a big smile.

'Eliza! What a surprise!'

'I'm not giving you a penny,' she said and walked past him.

But Alfred caught her arm. 'Now come on, Eliza. Just give your old dad a few pence for a drink on his way home.'

* Buckingham Palace: The home of the British queen (or king) in London.

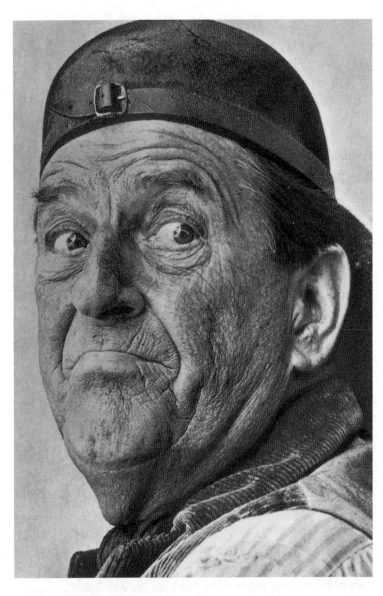

Alfred Doolittle, still wearing his dirty old work clothes, came out into the street, looking quite unhappy.

Eliza took some money from her pocket and looked at it. 'Well, I had a bit of luck tonight, so here.' She put the money in his hand. 'But don't think I'm going to give you something every day.' She went on down the street.

Immediately, arm in arm, Alfred and his friends turned and went back into the pub. 'George! Three beautiful beers, please!' And Alfred and his friends started singing happily.

Alfred:
The Lord above gave man an arm of iron
So he could do his job and never shirk.
The Lord above gave man an arm of iron – but
With a little bit of luck,
With a little bit of luck,
Someone else'll do the blinkin' work!

The three men together:
With a little bit . . . with a little bit . . .
With a little bit of luck
You'll never work!

Alfred:
The Lord above made liquor for temptation,
To see if man could turn away from sin.
The Lord above made liquor for temptation – but
With a little bit of luck,
With a little bit of luck,
When Temptation comes you'll give right in!

The three men together:
With a little bit . . . with a little bit . . .
With a little bit of luck
You'll give right in!

Alfred:

Oh, you can walk the straight and narrow;
But with a little bit of luck
You'll run amuck!
The gentle sex was made for man to marry,
To share his nest and see his food is cooked.
The gentle sex was made for man to marry – but
With a little bit of luck,
With a little bit of luck,
You can have it all and not get hooked.

The three men together:
With a little bit . . . with a little bit . . .
With a little bit of luck
You won't get hooked.
With a little bit . . . with a little bit . . .
With a little bit of luck
With a little bit of bloomin' luck!

A woman put her head out of an upstairs window further up the street and shouted, 'Shut up down there, will you? How do you think I can sleep with all that noise?'

'I'm trying to keep them quiet,' Alfred shouted back, and the three men moved off down the street, still singing, but a little more quietly.

Chapter 3   The Crazy Professor

The next morning Professor Higgins and his new friend, Colonel Pickering, were in the Professor's work-room in his flat. The Colonel was sitting in a comfortable armchair. The room was very dark but he could see a desk with untidy papers all over it and a telephone. Round the room there were different machines and pictures of mouths and lips and tongues on some of the walls. Other walls were full of lines of books – thousands of books. Strange sounds were coming from a small recording machine in one corner. Higgins was standing next to the machine, listening carefully.

'Can we have the lights on in a minute?' Pickering asked.

'Not yet,' Higgins answered. 'You can hear much better in the dark.'

'But I think I've heard enough strange noises for this morning. My head's going round and round with them.'

Just then, Mrs Pearce, the Professor's housekeeper, came in. 'Are you in here, Mr Higgins?'

'What is it, Mrs Pearce?' Higgins asked, and turned down the recording machine a little.

'A young woman wants to see you, sir.'

Higgins turned the machine off. 'A young woman! What does she want?' He switched on the light. 'Has she got an interesting accent? Show her up, Mrs Pearce.'

Mrs Pearce went out and returned after a minute with Eliza, who was wearing her best, cleanest clothes and a very large orange, blue and red hat. Pickering, a kind-hearted man, immediately felt quite sorry for her, but for Higgins she was just another person he could listen to and study.

'Oh,' he said when he turned and saw her – and he was clearly not very pleased to see her again – 'it's that girl I was listening to last night. That's no good – I've already got recordings of all those west London accents. I don't want to see you, young woman. Goodbye.'

But Eliza did not move. 'Don't be so rude. You haven't heard why I'm here yet, have you? You said you gave lessons to people, but if my money isn't good enough, I'll keep it.'

'Good enough for what?' Higgins asked.

'Good enough for *you*. I've come to have lessons, see? And I'll pay for them, too – make no mistake.'

Surprise showed on Higgins' face. 'Well! What can I say?'

'What about "Please sit down"?' Eliza answered. 'If you're a gentleman, that is. I'm bringing you business, aren't I?' Higgins was not amused. He turned to Pickering. 'Shall we ask this *thing* to sit down, or shall we throw it out of the window?'

Eliza thought that he really meant to throw her out of the window and she moved quickly towards the door. 'Ah-ah-oh-ow-ow-oo! You can't call me a "thing" when I've offered to pay you!' She turned to Pickering. 'I just want to learn to speak good English and he said he'll teach me. So here I am with my money, ready to pay for lessons, and he calls me a "thing"! That's not right, is it?'

'Sit down, then. Go on, sit down, girl! Do what I tell you,' Higgins said rudely. 'What's your name?'

'Eliza Doolittle.'

'And how much do you plan to pay me for the lessons?'

'Well, a friend of mine gets French lessons from a real French gentleman for eighteen pence an hour. But you're just going to teach me English, which I can speak already, so I won't give you more than twelve pence. Take it or leave it.'

Higgins turned to Pickering. 'You know, Pickering, twelve pence probably means the same to this young woman as sixty pounds means to you or me. That's not a bad offer, is it?'

'Sixty pounds! What are you talking about!' Eliza jumped up. 'I didn't offer you sixty pounds!'

'Oh, sit down and be quiet,' Higgins said.

Now Pickering spoke for the first time. 'I think it's a very interesting offer, Higgins. You know, if you can teach her to speak English without a London accent, and then take her to some of London's finest dances and parties without anyone knowing that she isn't really a lady, then I'll say that you're the greatest teacher in the world! Listen – I've got an offer for you, too: if you can do that, then I'll pay for all the costs of the girl's lessons. How's that?'

'Oh, you're a good man, you are, sir,' Eliza said to him.

Higgins was looking at her, starting to see that this was a very interesting idea. 'Mmm,' he said. 'She's so wonderfully *low*, so terribly *dirty* – I'll do it! I'll turn this *thing* into a real lady!'

'Aoooooow! I'm not dirty: I washed my face and hands before I came, you know.'

But Higgins was not listening. He was now quite excited by the plan. 'I'll start today! Now! This minute! Take her away and clean her, please, Mrs Pearce. Take off all her clothes and burn them, then order some new ones for her.'

'Take my clothes off? You're no gentleman, you're not, talking about things like that! I'm a good girl, I am.'

'Take her away, Mrs Pearce. If she gives you any trouble, hit her on her behind!'

'Aooooow! I'll call the police!'

'But, sir . . .' Mrs Pearce was starting to get worried about this idea. 'I haven't got a room for her. And you can't just take a girl off the street like this – you don't know anything about her! What about her parents? Or perhaps she's married.'

Eliza laughed. 'Me? Married? Men don't marry girls like me!'

'No, Eliza,' Higgins said, laughing loudly, 'but men will be shooting themselves in the streets, dying of their love for you, by the time I've finished with you!'

'He's strange – a bit wrong in the head, he is,' Eliza said. 'I don't think I want him teaching me . . .'

'Wrong in the head, am I? Mrs Pearce, forget everything I said about new clothes. Just throw her out, please.'

Mrs Pearce was not at all amused. 'Mr Higgins, please stop! This is not right. Go home to your parents, girl.'

'I haven't got any parents.'

Higgins was pleased. 'See? She hasn't got any parents. She doesn't belong to anybody. Take her upstairs and . . .'

But Mrs Pearce stopped him again. 'Mr Higgins. I must know what she's going to do here. What will happen to her when you've finished teaching her? What about that, sir?'

'When I've finished with her, we can throw her back into the street.'

'Oh, you've got no heart, have you?' Eliza said. 'You only think about yourself. I've had enough of this. I'm going.' She stood up.

Higgins took her arm and walked with her towards the window. 'Listen, Eliza. Think of riding in taxis, wearing gold and fine clothes . . . and I'll give you boxes of chocolates every day. You'll stay here for the next six months and learn to speak beautiful English. And at the end of the six months, you'll go to Buckingham Palace in a beautiful new dress, and you'll meet the King.' He turned to Mrs Pearce and Colonel Pickering. 'There! Are you happy now, Mrs Pearce?'

Mrs Pearce was not really very happy about it, but she turned to leave and said, 'Come with me, Eliza.'

Eliza walked to the door, then turned and said to Higgins. 'You're a bully, that's what you are. But you won't bully me, you know . . .' and she left the room.

'In a few months I'm going to turn that *thing* into a lady, a queen,' Higgins said quietly. 'She'll be able to go anywhere, mix with anyone. I'm not a bully – I'm a nice, ordinary, quiet man. I just don't think very much of women, that's all, and I like to live in *my* way. I've had a nice quiet time without women up to now, and no woman is ever going to change that!'

Chapter 4 The Rain in Spain

Alfred Doolittle was back at the pub near Covent Garden three days later, but again the barman was throwing him out. Again,

Alfred and his friends hadn't got enough money to pay for their drinks. A large, untidy London woman, who loved to talk about all the local news to anyone who listened, was sitting at the bar, watching.

'You can buy the drinks now, Alfred. You're a lucky man.'

'Me? Lucky? Why?'

'That daughter of yours, Eliza. She's living with a rich gentleman now, you know. Fine new clothes and riding about in taxis, and she asked me to send her things to 27a Wimpole Street – a Professor Higgins' place.'

Alfred was very pleased with the news. 'I always knew it! She's going to do well for herself, I always said. My friends, we're going to have a few drinks! At last the sun is shining on Alfred P. Doolittle!'

♦

Later that same afternoon, Higgins was in his work-room, at his flat. Pickering was there, too, reading the newspaper. Mrs Pearce came in. 'Mr Higgins,' she said, 'there's a man downstairs, Mr Alfred Doolittle. He wants to see you – he says you have his daughter here.'

'Send him up.'

Pickering looked up from his paper. 'I think we're going to have some trouble with him,' he said.

'I think *he's* going to have some trouble with *me*, not I with him,' Higgins answered.

Mrs Pearce came back. 'Mr Doolittle, sir.'

Alfred walked in, holding his hat. 'Professor Higgins?'

'Here!' Higgins was by the window.

'I've come about something very serious, sir. I want my daughter back. See?'

'Of course you want her back. She's your daughter, isn't she? She's upstairs. You can take her away immediately.'

This was not the answer Alfred wanted to hear. 'What?!'

'Take her away,' Higgins said. 'I'm not going to keep your daughter away from you. And don't try asking me for money because she's stayed here with us, or I'll call the police.'

'I haven't asked for a penny,' Alfred said. He turned to Pickering. 'Have I?'

But Higgins went on, 'Mrs Pearce, Eliza's father has come to take her away. Give her to him.'

'Now wait a minute, sir,' Alfred said. 'You and I are men of the world, aren't we? If you really want to keep Eliza here, maybe we can come to some agreement about it. I can see you're an honest sort of man – well, what's five pounds to you, and what's Eliza to me?'

'You know, Pickering, this is a clever man, with a very clever tongue. I think I'm going to give him ten pounds, not just five,' Higgins said and put his hand into his pocket.

'Oh no, sir,' Alfred said, 'not ten pounds. You give me what I asked for, and not a penny more. See, with five pounds I can go out for a good evening with my lady-love, and we'll be perfectly happy.'

Higgins put five pounds into Alfred's hand.

'Oh, thank you, sir,' Alfred said and hurried towards the door. Just then, the door flew open and a well-dressed, clean, but very angry young woman stormed in, waving a book in front of her and almost knocking Alfred over with it.

'I won't! I won't! I won't!' she shouted. 'I won't say those stupid sounds one more time!' Then she saw her father and looked more angry than ever. 'What are *you* doing here?'

'You hold your tongue, my girl,' Alfred answered, 'and don't give these gentlemen any trouble, ever. You hear?' Then he turned politely to Higgins and Pickering. 'Good afternoon, sirs,' he said, and he went out of the door, laughing.

'There's a clever man for you,' Higgins said, smiling.

'What did he come here for?' Eliza asked, still angry.

'Just say those sounds again,' was Higgins' answer.

Eliza shouted the sounds at him. 'Ahyee, Eeee, Iyee, Ow, You! I've said them again and again for the last three days, and I won't say them again! You haven't got a heart!'

'Eliza,' Higgins said quietly, 'you will learn to pronounce those sounds in the right way before this evening, or you will have no supper and no chocolates!' And he walked out, closing the door hard behind him.

Eliza threw the book on the floor and jumped up and down on it, shouting, 'Just you wait, Henry Higgins! Just you wait! You'll be sorry – I'll pay you back for this!'

♦

The day went past. Eliza practised and practised different sounds and words, all day, every day. Higgins gave her sentences to say, with difficult sounds in them: *The rain in Spain stays mainly in the plain* and *In Hertford, Hereford and Hampshire, hurricanes hardly ever happen* and *How kind of you to let me come*. But Eliza couldn't say them in the right way, so she had to repeat them fifty times ... sixty times ... a hundred times! Higgins asked her to try saying things with small stones in her mouth and one went down her throat by mistake. He asked her to say things while he played music. Eliza tried and tried, but she was never good enough.

'*The rain in Spain stays mainly in the plain,*' Higgins said at the end of one long evening. It was very late.

'I can't,' Eliza said. 'I'm so tired. I'm so tired.'

'I know you're tired, Eliza,' Higgins said, his voice suddenly kind. 'But think of what you're trying to learn – the beautiful English language! It's the greatest thing we have – and you *will* learn it. Now, try again.'

Slowly Eliza tried again. '*The rain in Spain stays mainly in the plain.*' She pronounced it perfectly!

17

The rain in Spain stays mainly in the plain!

Higgins sat up straight in his chair. 'What did you say?'

Eliza repeated it, again perfectly, with no London accent at all! Higgins stood up. He couldn't believe his ears.

'Again.'

Eliza started to sing the sentence and soon Higgins and Pickering were singing with her.

Eliza: *The rain in Spain stays mainly in the plain.*
Higgins: *I think she's got it! I think she's got it!*
Eliza: *The rain in Spain stays mainly in the plain.*
Higgins: *By George, she's got it! By George, she's got it! Now once again, where does it rain?*
Eliza: *On the plain! On the plain!*
Higgins: *And where's that soggy plain?*
Eliza: *In Spain! In Spain!*
Pickering jumped to his feet and they all sang together:

The rain in Spain stays mainly in the plain!
The rain in Spain stays mainly in the plain!
Higgins tried another sentence: *In Hertford, Hereford and Hampshire . . . ?*
Eliza: *Hurricanes hardly happen.*
Then she sang another one: *How kind of you to let me come!*
Higgins: *Now once again, where does it rain?*
Eliza: *On the plain! On the plain!*
Higgins: *And where's that blasted plain?*
Eliza: *In Spain! In Spain!*
And they all sang together:
The rain in Spain stays mainly in the plain!
The rain in Spain stays mainly in the plain!

Higgins took Eliza in his arms and they danced round the room together, until they fell on the sofa, laughing.

'Pickering,' Higgins said, 'I think the time has come to take her out to meet other people and see how she does. We must buy her a new dress – nothing too flowery, of course.'

The door opened slowly and Mrs Pearce, with a worried face, looked into the room. 'Is everything all right, sir? There was a terrible noise from down here.'

'Everything is wonderful, thank you, Mrs Pearce. Eliza, you go on with your work,' Higgins answered, and he went out. Pickering followed him.

'Work? At this time of night?' Mrs Pearce said. 'Eliza, it doesn't matter what Mr Higgins says, you must go to bed.'

But Eliza was so happy, she just wanted to sing.

> *Bed! Bed! I couldn't go to bed!*
> *My head's too light to try to set it down!*
> *Sleep! Sleep! I couldn't sleep tonight!*
> *Not for all the jewels in the crown!*

But Eliza was so happy she just wanted to sing...
I could have danced all night!

I could have danced all night!
I could have danced all night!
And still have begged for more.
I could have spread my wings
And done a thousand things
I've never done before.

I'll never know
What made it so exciting;
Why all at once
My heart took flight.
I only know when he
Began to dance with me,
I could have danced, danced, danced all night!

Chapter 5   In Love at the Races

It was a sunny June afternoon for the horse races at Ascot, near London. Pickering was there in his best black suit and hat, and with him was Mrs Higgins. She looked worried.

'Colonel Pickering, do you mean that my son is coming to Ascot today? That's an unpleasant surprise, you know – Ascot is the one place I can come with my friends without meeting Henry. When my friends do meet him, I never see them again.'

'He had to come, Mrs Higgins. You see, he's taking the girl to the big Embassy Ball soon, and he wanted to take her somewhere to meet people first.'

'What girl?'

'Oh, didn't I say? Miss Doolittle – she lives with Henry.'

'Lives with Henry? Is he in love with her?'

'Oh no! Nothing like that! She's a flower girl, from the street. He's trying to teach her to speak good English.'

'But Colonel, are you saying that Henry is bringing a flower girl here, to Ascot?'

'Yes, Mrs Higgins! That's right! Very good, Mrs Higgins!'

◆

Higgins was among the crowds watching the races when he met his mother a few minutes later.

'I hear you've brought a flower girl from Covent Garden to Ascot with you, Henry,' she said. 'Is that true?'

'Oh, mother dear, she'll be all right. She's only going to talk about the weather. Perhaps you can help her a bit?'

Just then, Freddy Eynsford-Hill and his mother came across to say hello to Mrs Higgins, and Pickering arrived with Eliza. She was wearing a wonderful dress and looked very beautiful. Freddy couldn't take his eyes off her. He was immediately, hopelessly in love with her.

Pickering arrived with Eliza. She was wearing a wonderful dress and looked very beautiful.

'The first race was very exciting, Miss Doolittle. Did you see it?' he asked her.

'The rain in Spain stays mainly in the plain,' Eliza said. 'But in Hertford, Hereford and Hampshire, hurricanes hardly ever happen.'

Freddy thought this was very funny, but soon Eliza started to talk about things that she did not know how to say and her London accent came back to her. Mrs Higgins did not know what to do – all her fine friends were listening with surprised faces. Higgins and Pickering tried to stop Eliza and finally Pickering took Eliza by the arm and said, 'Come along, my dear. Let's go and watch the next race, shall we?'

But Mrs Higgins stopped him. 'You can watch the race from here, Colonel.'

'I've got some money on a horse called Dover – it's number seven in this race,' Freddy said to Eliza. 'Here, please take my ticket for it – it's yours.'

Eliza took the ticket. 'How kind of you,' she said.

The race started and the horses ran. At first Eliza just said 'Come on, Dover!' quite quietly, but then she got more and more excited. Her London accent got stronger and stronger, until she was shouting, 'Come on, Dover! Move your fat behind!' in her loudest voice. Pickering quickly left and Higgins started to laugh and laugh.

♦

That evening Freddy was in Wimpole Street. Smiling, he knocked on the door of 27a. Mrs Pearce opened it and Freddy asked if Miss Doolittle was at home. He gave Mrs Pearce some flowers for Eliza and said that he would wait.

'Don't hurry,' he said. 'I want to drink in this street where she lives.' And he turned to look lovingly at the street. A song came into his head and he sang while he waited.

23

Eliza's London accent got stronger and stronger, until she was shouting,
'Come on, Dover! Move your fat behind!' in her loudest voice.

I have often walked down this street before;
But the pavement always stayed beneath my feet before.
All at once am I
Several storeys high,
Knowing I'm on the street where you live.

Are there lilac trees in the heart of town?
Can you hear a lark in any other part of town?
Does enchantment pour
Out of every door?
No, it's just on the street where you live!

And oh, the towering feeling
Just to know somehow you are near!
The overpowering feeling
That any second you may suddenly appear!

24

People stop and stare. They don't bother me.
For there's nowhere else on earth that I would rather be.
Let the time go by,
I won't care if I
Can be here on the street where you live.

The door opened again. Mrs Pearce looked out. 'Mr Eynsford-Hill? I'm very sorry, sir, but Miss Doolittle says that she never wants to see anyone ever again.'

'But why? She was wonderful! Tell her I'll wait.'

'But, sir, maybe it'll be days . . . or weeks!'

'But don't you see? I'll be happier here,' Freddy said, and he sang the last part of his song again:

People stop and stare. They don't bother me.
For there's nowhere else on earth that I would rather be.
Let the time go by,
I won't care if I
Can be here on the street where you live.

Then he sat down outside Eliza's front door to wait.

Chapter 6   A Real Lady

One evening, six weeks later, Higgins and Pickering were in Higgins' work-room at the flat in Wimpole Street. They were both in black evening suits, ready to go out.

'What happens if she makes another terrible mistake at the Embassy Ball tonight, Higgins?'

'There are no horses at the Ball, Pickering. Stop worrying.'

Mrs Pearce came in. 'The car is here, sir.'

A few minutes later Eliza walked into the room, looking very

25

beautiful in an expensive new evening dress. Pickering stood up, his mouth open.

'Miss Doolittle, you look beautiful.'

'Thank you, Colonel Pickering.'

Higgins studied Eliza carefully. Then he said, 'Not bad. Not bad at all.'

Pickering, always gentlemanly, offered Eliza his arm and they went downstairs together, to the car.

♦

They arrived at the Ball and a doorman called their names when they walked into the ballroom. Mrs Higgins immediately came over for a word with Colonel Pickering.

'People think she's charming, Mrs Higgins,' he told her. 'Lady Tarrington asked me who that beautiful young woman with Professor Higgins was and I had to think for a minute before I said "Eliza Doolittle".'

'That was very quick of you Colonel. You know, she *is* charming. I've come to like that girl so much in the last few weeks. Where is she?'

'Upstairs,' Pickering answered at the same time as the doorman called out, 'Miss Eliza Doolittle', and Eliza came down the stairs to the ballroom. Everybody in the room turned to watch her. Higgins moved to meet her at the bottom of the stairs.

Then the Queen of Transylvania came into the room with her husband and, walking past Eliza, she stopped and put one hand up to touch Eliza's face.

'Charming,' she said. 'Absolutely charming.' And she moved on into the room.

The music began and people moved on to the dance-floor in pairs. Higgins took Eliza on to the dance-floor and they danced away together among the other dancers.

♦

The music began and people moved on to the dance-floor in pairs.

They arrived home from the Ball at three o'clock in the morning. Eliza was tired. She stood quietly near Higgins' desk in the corner while Higgins and Pickering talked excitedly together.

'You did it, Higgins! You did it! Well done!'

Eliza stood without moving and listened. She got more and more angry. At last, when Pickering left the room and Higgins told her to bring him his slippers, she could not stop herself. The slippers were by his desk; she picked them up and threw them at him, shouting, 'There are your slippers . . . and there!'

'What's the matter with you? What's wrong?' asked Higgins, very surprised.

'Nothing's wrong – with *you*. *You* did it, didn't you?' she shouted at Higgins. '*You* did it! What about *me*? Didn't I do it too? But I don't matter, do I? I'd like to kill you, you big-headed bully! You're just pleased that it's all finished now, aren't you? Now you can throw me back on the street!' Eliza tried to hit him on the side of the face, but he caught her arm and pushed her down on to the sofa.

'You want to hit me, do you? Just sit down and be quiet.'

Eliza sat, feeling sad and hopeless. 'What's going to happen to me now?' she asked, and she started to cry.

'Does it matter what happens to you?' Higgins answered angrily. 'Are you suddenly saying that I haven't been good to you? That I haven't helped you? . . . Perhaps you're just tired after the Ball. Have a chocolate. There's nothing more to worry about now.'

'Nothing more to worry about. I'd like to be dead,' Eliza said quietly. 'I heard you say "Thank God it's all finished!" What do I do now? Where do I go?'

'Oh, that's what you're worrying about, is it? I don't think you'll have any trouble finding a good job now, you know. Perhaps marry someone – you see Eliza, not all men dislike women, like I do. Go to bed and have a good night's sleep and you'll see everything differently in the morning, I'm sure. Perhaps my mother can find a nice young man for you to marry. But I'm tired now, too. I must go to bed.' He walked to the door and went out.

Eliza fell on to a chair and started to cry again.

Chapter 7   Married in the Morning

Some time later, Eliza came quietly out of the front door of the house, carrying a small suitcase. Freddy was still there, having been there every day, only leaving to eat, sleep and change his clothes. He didn't see Eliza immediately, but then he did . . .

'My love!' he cried.

'What are you doing here?'

'Oh, nothing much. I spend most of my time here. This is the only place I . . . You know I'm in love with you, Eliza!'

Freddy said, 'I . . . You know I'm in love with you, Eliza!'
Eliza had no time for this.

Eliza had no time for this. She walked off down the street, with Freddy behind her, saying, 'My love . . . my love!'

♦

It was five o'clock, early in the morning of that same night. The fruit and flower sellers at Covent Garden market were just starting their day's work and a few of them were near a small fire again, talking and keeping warm. Some of them were singing a few lines of Eliza's song: . . . *Warm face, warm hands, warm feet . . . Oh, wouldn't it be loverly?*

Eliza came into the square and walked shyly over to the fire. The men stopped singing.

'Good morning, Miss. Can we help you?' They did not know who she was. Then one of them looked at her closely.

'Yes?' Eliza asked.

'Sorry, Miss,' the man said, 'for a minute I thought you were somebody I knew. . . Can I get you a taxi?'

'No, thank you,' Eliza answered sadly.

Suddenly the door of a pub on the side of the square opened and Eliza's father came out. He was wearing a new black morning suit, with shining black shoes.

'Father!' Eliza said.

Alfred stopped and turned. 'Oh no! She's come back to spy on me, my girl has!'

'Come along now, Alfred,' one of his friends said and took him by the arm. 'We've got to get you to the church.'

'Church?' Eliza asked.

'Yes, church,' her father answered. 'That's the terrible thing. Why do you think I'm wearing all these fine clothes? My lady-love wants to marry me, now that I've got some money. That's why. You can come and see them finish me off this morning, if you want – St George's Church, Hanover Square at ten o'clock.'

30

The crowd lifted Alfred above their heads and carried him off towards the church.

'No, thank you, Dad. But good luck.' She turned and slowly left the square.

Alfred turned to his friends. 'How much time have I still got?' he asked. 'There are drinks and girls all over London, and I must find some of them in the next few hours!' And he suddenly started to sing.

> *I'm getting married in the morning!*
> *Ding dong! The bells are gonna chime.*
> *Pull out the stopper!*
> *Let's have a whopper!*
> *But get me to the church on time!*
>
> *I gotta be there in the mornin'*
> *Spruced up and lookin' in me prime.*

31

Girls, come and kiss me;
Show how you'll miss me.
But get me to the church on time!
If I am dancin'
Roll up the floor.
If I am whistlin'
Whewt me out the door!

For I'm getting married in the mornin'
Ding dong! The bells are gonna chime.
Kick up a rumpus
But don't lose the compass;
And get me to the church,
Get me to the church,
For Gawd's sake, get me to the church on time!

Alfred and all his friends started to sing and dance a final 'goodbye' dance for Alfred all through the market. The sun was almost up now. It was morning.

The crowd lifted Alfred above their heads and carried him off towards the church.

Chapter 8   A Sad Day for Higgins

Back at Higgins' flat, at about eleven o'clock that same morning, Higgins was shouting from his room. 'Pickering! Pickering! Eliza's gone!'

Pickering came in. 'Gone?'

'Yes. Gone! Run away! What am I going to do? I can't find where anything is and I don't know who's coming to see me this morning. Eliza knew all that, but she's gone.'

'Higgins, did you bully her again last night? Is that why she's run away?' Pickering asked.

'Just the opposite – she bullied me. She threw my slippers at me. I don't understand it – we were so good to her. Please, Pickering, do something! Call the police! I want to find her! She belongs to me! I paid five pounds for her!'

'The police? Good idea.' Pickering picked up the phone.

Higgins went on, 'Why did she go? I can't understand it at all! Women are never sensible! They've got heads full of wool, stupid things! Why can't women be more like men, that's what I want to know? Why can't women be like *us*?'

♦

At about the same time, Eliza was at Mrs Higgins' house.

'You mean that you did this wonderful thing for them at the Ball, without one mistake, and they never said how wonderful you were? Never said thank you?' Mrs Higgins asked.

Higgins went on, 'Why did she go? I can't understand it at all! Women are never sensible! . . . Why can't women be more like men, that's what I want to know?'

33

'Not a word,' Eliza answered.

'That's terrible, my dear. Really terrible!'

Eliza started to smile, but her smile quickly disappeared when she heard Higgins' voice from the front door.

'Mother! Mother!'

'Stay where you are, my dear,' Mrs Higgins said to Eliza.

'Mother! The most terrible thing has happened . . .' Higgins said, hurrying into the room. He stopped when he saw Eliza.

'You!' he shouted.

'How are you, Professor Higgins. Quite well, I hope?' Eliza said. 'Will you have a cup of tea?'

'Don't you try that game on me!' Higgins shouted back. 'I taught you! Now get up and come home and stop being so stupid! You've given me enough trouble for one morning!'

'Very polite, Henry! What a nice way to ask a young lady to come to your house!' Mrs Higgins said to her son. 'Now you be polite to Eliza or I'll ask you to leave. Why don't you talk to her about the weather or something?' Then Mrs Higgins turned and left them together.

Higgins sat down and took a cup of tea.

'Well, Eliza, you've paid me back now. Have you finished? Or do you want more? I'll be quite all right without you, you know . . .' But then his voice changed, 'But I will miss you, Eliza. You've taught me a few things, too.'

'You've got my voice on your recording machine. You can turn that on any time you want to hear me, and you can't hurt machines, can you? What do you want me back for?'

'Oh, I see,' Higgins answered. 'You want me to be in love with you or something, do you? Like Freddy? Is that it?'

Eliza did not know what to say for a minute. Then she said, 'No, that's not it. I just want you to be kinder to me. I stayed with you, not for the new dresses and the taxis, but because we were *pleasant* together. I felt friendly towards you.'

'Yes, of course. Well, Pickering and I feel the same. You're being stupid.'

'Oh! I can't talk to you: you turn everything against me. I'll marry Freddy, that's what I'll do. He loves me.'

'Freddy! Freddy is a good for nothing! Woman, you don't understand! I have taught you to be a real lady – you can't go and marry a man like Freddy!'

Eliza just laughed at him. 'Or perhaps I'll be a teacher – I'll teach phonetics. I don't like your big talk and your bullying, you see, Henry Higgins! You're not the beginning and the end! The world will still go round without you, you know! There'll still be rain down on that plain in Spain without you! I can look after myself without you!'

Higgins just sat and looked at her. 'Eliza, you're wonderful! I like you to be strong like this!'

Eliza looked at him coldly, turned away and walked to the door. 'Goodbye, Professor Higgins. I won't be seeing you again.' She went.

Higgins could not speak. He walked slowly to the door and called weakly. 'Mother! Mother!'

His mother came in. 'What is it, Henry? What's happened?'

'She's gone,' he said, almost to himself. 'What can I do?'

Chapter 9   Where Are My Slippers?

Higgins was outside his house in Wimpole Street late that afternoon. He couldn't stop thinking about Eliza. Now he knew that he wanted her with him. She was part of his world.

> *I've grown accustomed to her face!*
> *She almost makes the day begin.*
> *I've grown accustomed to the tune*
> *She whistles night and noon.*

35

Higgins was outside his house in Wimpole Street late that afternoon.
He couldn't stop thinking about Eliza . . .
I've grown accustomed to her face!

Her smiles. Her frowns.
Her ups, her downs,
Are second nature to me now;
Like breathing out and breathing in.
I was serenely independent and content before we met;
Surely I could always be that way again — and yet
I've grown accustomed to her looks;
Accustomed to her voice:
Accustomed to her face.

He stopped singing. 'Marry Freddy!' he said angrily. 'What a stupid idea! What a heartless thing to do! She won't be happy. She'll come knocking on my door one night . . . I'm really a most forgiving man . . . but I'll *never* take her back! Never! Marry Freddy! Ha!'

He took his key out of his pocket but suddenly stopped. He did not know quite what to do without Eliza. He needed her.

♦

He was in his work-room that evening, but he couldn't work. He walked round and round the room. He stopped next to his recording machine and turned it on. Eliza's voice came out into the room. He sat down with his back to the machine and listened, his head down.

'I washed my face and hands before I came, you know,' Eliza said.

'I want to be a lady in a flower shop,' her voice said, 'instead of selling flowers at the corner of Tottenham Court Road. He said he could teach me, but he bullies me all the time.'

Very softly Eliza walked into the room behind him. She stood looking at him.

'She was so wonderfully *low*, so terribly *dirty*,' Higgins said sadly to himself, remembering her first visit to this room.

Eliza turned off the machine. 'I washed my face and hands before I came, you know,' she said.

Higgins sat up straight in his chair. Most of all he wanted to laugh loudly, to run to her. Instead, he sat back in the chair again, pushed his hat down over his eyes and very softly said, 'Eliza, where are my slippers?'

Eliza wanted to cry. She understood him so well.

ACTIVITIES

Chapter 1

Before you read

1 Look at the Word List at the back of the book. Answer these questions with words from the list. Who:

    a orders the food and cleans in a rich person's house?

    b opens the door for you when you arrive at an expensive hotel?

    c teaches at a university?

    d hurts weaker people?

    e is always polite and charming?

2 Find words on the Word List to complete these sentences.

    a 'That rude child is sticking her ..... out at me!'

    b 'Get inside! Shut the doors and windows! A ..... is coming!'

    c 'Someone just stole my passport!'

       'Go to your country's ..... to get a new one.'

    d 'I am ..... sure that I have met you somewhere before. I know your face so well.'

    e 'We ..... go abroad on holiday – we usually stay in Britain.'

    f 'My feet are cold! Where are my .....?'

    g 'There's a university ..... at the end of the summer term.'

    h 'His ..... is so strong that I can't understand him.'

    i 'Because my name starts with the last letter of the ....., I'm always last.'

3 Read the Introduction to the book. Answer these questions.

    a How and where does Eliza Doolittle earn money?

    b Why can't she have a better life?

    c Who thinks he can change her?

    d Were there any songs in the 1912 play?

While you read

4 Underline the things that are wrong. Write the right words.

    a It's March. It's cold. It's in the morning.

       It's a square in central London.   ....

b Freddy is 20, he's rich and he's looking for
his mother. ....

c Eliza is young, she's a dancer and she's
wearing old, dirty clothes. ....

d Freddy's mother pays for the flowers that
Freddy knocked on the ground. ....

e The crowd think the man with the little
book is a writer. ....

f The gentleman comes from west London. ....

g Eliza is polite to the gentleman. ....

h Colonel Pickering and Professor Higgins
have met before. ....

i Colonel Pickering writes books about
phonetics. ....

j Professor Higgins invites Eliza to 27a
Wimpole Street. ....

After you read

5 Which of these things is not happening in Covent Garden at the
beginning of the story?
- street musicians are singing and dancing
- theatre-goers are going home
- rich Londoners are looking for taxis
- fruit- and vegetable-sellers are waiting to start work
- it's snowing

6 Talk to other students. Discuss these questions.
  a Do you know what a London accent sounds like?
  b What is your favourite accent in your language?
  c Are there 'good' and 'bad' accents in your language?
  d Can you say some sentences in different accents? What do
  your friends think of your accent – good or bad?

Chapters 2–3

Before you read

7 Work with another student. Have this conversation.

   Student A: You were in the crowd in Covent Garden last night. Tell your friend about Eliza and the strange gentleman.

   Student B: Listen to your friend and ask questions about what happened.

8 Chapter 3 is called 'The Crazy Professor'.

   What will be 'crazy' about Professor Higgins, do you think?

While you read

9 Choose the best answers.

   a What is most important to Alfred?
   * drinking with his friends   * doing a good day's work
   * spending time with his daughter

   b Why are Alfred and his friends making so much noise?
   * they love singing   * they've had too many drinks
   * they've heard good news

   c Why does Higgins turn his recording machine off?
   * Colonel Pickering has heard enough
   * a young woman arrives
   * Mrs Pearce asks him to turn it off

   d Why has Eliza come to see Professor Higgins?
   * she wants to sell him flowers   * she wants French lessons
   * she wants to learn to speak good English

   e How much does she offer to pay for each lesson?
   * twelve pence   * eighteen pence   * sixty pounds

   f How does Higgins speak to Eliza?
   * politely   * rudely   * very rudely

   g What does Mrs Pearce think of the professor's plan?
   * she likes it   * she doesn't like it
   * she thinks it's interesting

   h What does the professor call Eliza?
   * a queen   * a lady   * a thing

After you read

10 What are the missing names?

    a ..... wants to know: is ..... really a very clever teacher?

    b ..... thinks ..... is wrong in the head.

    c ..... thinks ..... should go home to her parents.

    d ..... thinks ..... will meet the King in six months.

Chapter 4

Before you read

11 Discuss these questions.

    a At the end of Chapter 3, Professor Higgins says, 'I like to live in my way … no woman is ever going to change that.' Do you think he will change or not?

    b Chapter 4 is called 'The Rain in Spain'. Why, do you think?

While you read

12 Are these sentences right (✓) or wrong (✗)?

    a When Eliza's father hears that she is living in Wimpole Street, he orders more drinks in the pub. .....

    b Alfred Doolittle really wants his daughter back from Professor Higgins. .....

    c The professor gives Alfred ten pounds. .....

    d Alfred is more interested in the money than in his daughter. .....

    e Eliza doesn't practise very hard. .....

    f Eliza has to practise speaking with stones in her mouth. .....

    g In the end, Eliza says 'the rain in Spain' perfectly. .....

    h The professor thinks Eliza is ready to meet rich people. .....

After you read

13 Work with another student. Have this conversation.

    Student A: You are Alfred Doolittle after your visit to Professor Higgins. Tell your friend all about Wimpole Street and the money, and buy drinks for everyone.

    Student B: You are Alfred's friend. Listen to his story and ask questions.

Chapters 5–6

Before you read

14 Eliza is ready to go and meet people. Which of these things will happen, do you think?

   a Everyone will think Eliza is a beautiful young lady.

   b Eliza will forget all her lessons and go back to her old accent.

   c Eliza's old street friends will come and talk to her in front of the rich people.

While you read

15 Circle the correct words in *italics*.

   a Mrs Higgins *is / isn't* pleased that Henry has come to Ascot.

   b Mrs Higgins's friends *do / don't* like her son.

   c Professor Higgins *thinks / doesn't think* Eliza is going to say a lot at the races.

   d When the horses are running, Eliza shouts in her *old / new* accent.

   e Eliza tells *the horse / Mrs Higgins* to move her fat behind.

   f Freddy brings flowers for *Mrs Pearce / Eliza*.

   g Eliza *agrees / refuses* to see Freddy.

   h Colonel Pickering nearly *remembers / forgets* Eliza's name because she looks so different.

   i Professor Higgins dances with *the Queen of Transylvania / Eliza*.

   j Eliza throws the slippers at *Pickering / Higgins*.

   k Eliza *knows / doesn't know* what she will do now.

   l Professor Higgins *is / isn't* interested in what happens to Eliza next.

After you read

16 Work with other students. You are at the Embassy Ball. You are watching everything that goes on. You don't know who Eliza Doolittle is. Talk about her, the ball, the Queen of Transylvania, the dancing, the drinks, the food. Discuss all the things that happen.

Chapters 7–9

Before you read

17 Which of the following do you think will happen?

    a Eliza will be a flower-seller in Covent Garden again.

    b She will marry Freddy.

    c She will marry Colonel Pickering.

    d Something else will happen. What?

While you read

18 Put these words in the correct spaces below.

calls the police	Eliza is sad
walks away	girls and drinks
He can't work	He is angry
Henry is surprised	outside the house

    a Freddy is .... because he is in love with Eliza.

    b Eliza .... because she isn't in love with Freddy.

    c .... because she doesn't belong in Covent Garden any more.

    d Alfred is looking for .... because he is getting married later.

    e Pickering .... because Eliza has gone.

    f .... because Eliza is at his mother's house.

    g .... because Eliza is going to marry Freddy.

    h .... because he needs Eliza.

After you read

19 Talk to other students. Discuss these questions.

    a Is this story possible in your country now?

    b Was it possible in the past?

    c If the professor and Eliza stay together, will they have a happy life?

    d Is the professor a bully? How? Will he stop being a bully if he marries Eliza?

20 How much can you remember? Answer the questions. Look back through the book if necessary.

   a What is Eliza's job when the story starts?

   b Where do Professor Higgins and Eliza Doolittle first meet?

   c Who lives at 27a Wimpole Street?

   d Who is the professor's housekeeper?

   e What things hardly ever happen in Hertford, Hereford and Hampshire?

   f Complete Eliza's practice sentence: *The ..... in ..... stays mainly in the ..... .*

   g What happens at Ascot every June?

   h What happens to Freddy at Ascot this June?

   i Where does the Queen of Transylvania see Eliza?

Writing

21 Imagine a different ending. Eliza goes from Mrs Higgins's house to Wimpole Street and finds Freddy. She tells Professor Higgins that she is going to marry Freddy. Write the new ending.

22 It is six months later. Colonel Pickering has returned to India. Professor Higgins and Eliza write to their friend and tell him all their news. Write their letter.

23 Mrs Pearce has watched Eliza change from a street seller to a lady. Mrs Pearce's daughter comes to visit and she tells her about the last six months in Professor Higgins's house. Write their conversation.

24 Are there different accents in your country? Find out about them and describe them.

25 There are seven songs in the book. Write a sentence to explain why each person sings their song.

   Example: *Eliza, page 6: She's dreaming about a better life.*

26 *My Fair Lady* is a musical. Choose a musical film or play that you have seen. Think of something funny or sad that happens in it. Write a few sentences to tell the story.

27 Choose one of the photographs in the book and write about it. Who is in it? What is happening? What has just happened? What is going to happen next?

28 Imagine what Eliza's life is like at the beginning of the story. Compare it with her life at the end of the story. Decide which life you would prefer to live.

29 *My Fair Lady* (1958) comes from the older story of *Pygmalion* (1912), and this comes from an even older story. Each writer changed the story to make it modern for the 1900s. Can you change the story again and make it modern for the 2000s? Tell your story in a few sentences.

30 Imagine you are putting *My Fair Lady* on the theatre stage. Which actors will you choose for each part? What things will you have on stage to show the different places: Covent Garden, the professor's work-room, the races, the ball, Wimpole Street?

WORD LIST

absolutely (adv) completely

accent (n) a way of saying words that is different in different places

alphabet (n) all the letters of a language, for example abc-z

ball (n) a big party with dancing and everyone in their best clothes

bully (n/v) a person who tries to frighten or hurt weaker people

charming (adj) very pleasing

Colonel (n) a title for a soldier with many officers and other soldiers under him

doorman (n) a man who works at the door of a hotel or theatre and helps people coming in or out

embassy (n) a building for the people who speak and act for a foreign government

gentleman (n) a man who is polite and honest and, usually, well-dressed

hardly ever (adv) almost never

housekeeper (n) a person who does the cooking and cleaning in another person's home

hurricane (n) a storm with a very strong and fast wind

lip (n) the redder or darker skin above or below the mouth

phonetics (n) the study of speech sounds

Professor (n) the most important or one of the most important teachers of a subject at a university

pronounce (v) to make the sound of a word or letter

slipper (n) a bedroom shoe

tongue (n) the soft moveable part in your mouth that you use for tasting and speaking

universal (adj) for everybody in the world

Notes on the songs

Use your dictionary to check the meaning of any of the words below that you do not know, or any of the words in the songs which have no notes.

1 ***Wouldn't It Be Loverly?*** (Eliza, page 6)
enormous = very big
loverly = lovely = very nice, very pleasant
choc'late = chocolate
makin' = making
sittin' = sitting
absobloominlutely two words mixed together
   1. absolutely 2. blooming = very (an English slang word, not very polite)
budge = move
winder sill = window sill (= the outside of a window)
restin' = resting
tender = kind and loving

2 ***With A Little Bit of Luck*** (Alfred Doolittle and friends, page 9)
the Lord above = God
an arm of iron = a very strong arm
shirk = to try not to do something difficult or unpleasant (e.g. hard work)
blinkin' means almost the same as *bloomin'* in the last song – it is also a slang
   word
liquor = strong drink, alcohol
temptation = wanting to do something that you know is wrong or stupid
sin = something you do that is bad or wrong
you'll give right in = you'll immediately stop fighting against something
   (e.g. a temptation) or somebody
walk the straight and narrow = live in a good, honest way
run amuck = go wrong, make a bad mistake (e.g. sin)
the gentle sex = women
share his nest = live with him
hooked = caught, married

3 ***The Rain In Spain*** (Eliza, with Higgins and Pickering, page 18)
plain = a large piece of open land with no hills and very few trees
By George...! = a way of saying that you are very surprised, like
   My Goodness! or *I don't believe it!*

soggy = very wet

hurricane = a storm with very strong winds

hardly = almost never

blasted = very windy; people also sometimes use this word with a slang meaning = very unpleasant

4 ***I Could Have Danced All Night*** (Eliza, page 19)

jewels = very expensive, colourful stones; people put them in gold rings, for example

crown = a gold thing with jewels in it which kings or queens sometimes wear on their head

begged = asked

spread my wings = started to fly like a bird

took flight = started to fly

5 ***On The Street Where You Live*** (Freddy, page 24)

pavement = the part of the side of the road where people walk

storeys = the floors of a tall building

lilac trees = trees with beautiful, sweet-smelling white, purple or pink flowers

a lark = a small bird which sings beautifully

enchantment = the feeling that everything is wonderful

towering = very big and strong

overpowering = very strong

stare = look for a long time

6 ***Get Me To The Church On Time*** (Alfred Doolittle, page 30)

'Ding dong!' are words which sound like a church bell

gonna = going to

chime = make the sound of a bell

stopper = the thing inside the neck of a bottle of beer or wine, it stops the beer or wine from coming out

a whopper = something very big – here, a big drink

I gotta = I have got to, I must

spruced up = very tidy

lookin' in me prime = looking as good as possible

whistlin' = whistling = making music through your lips

'Whewt' is not a real English word – Alfred uses this for the whistling noise; he means *hurry me (out of the door)*

kick up a rumpus = make a lot of trouble

compass = the thing which travellers use to find their way across deserts or the sea – it always points to the north, so, with a map, you know where you are going

Gawd's = God's; *For Gawd's sake* means the same here as *Please don't forget to...!*

7   ***I've Grown Accustomed To Her Face*** (Higgins, page 35)

accustomed to = when you are 'accustomed to' something, it is not strange to you; you know it very well

tune = the music of a song, without the words; people often whistle tunes

frown = people 'frown' when they are not pleased or angry – they pull their eyebrows together

second nature = not at all strange

serenely independent = quietly happy to be free

content = happy

looks = what her face looks like